Over the past few years, there has been growing concern — on the part of the American public as well as elected officials — about the tendency to sacrifice the nation's long-term interests in favor of short-term comfort and convenience. A recent *Washington Post* headline captured that habit in a phrase: "The Future Be Damned." The most worrisome example is the nation's $4 trillion public debt, which is growing at the staggering rate of almost $1 billion a day.

Since, at any given moment, the cure for deficit spending seems worse than the disease, leaders have repeatedly tried to avoid the problem and minimize its corrosive effects. On various occasions, the public has been told that if we can regain robust economic activity the nation can grow out of the problem.

But as the Clinton administration took office in 1993, it was readily apparent that the problem has been getting worse and that the nation will *not* grow out of it. In his confirmation hearing as budget director, Leon Panetta remarked that "We're looking at a deficit line that's shooting straight up. The new administration's task is to turn that curve back down. To make our economy more productive and provide greater opportunity for our children, the country needs to make tough choices and be prepared for some sacrifice."

Before the new administration had spent a dime on new programs, it faced a projected deficit of $310 billion, an all-time high. To close that huge budget gap will require some tough choices and an unusual degree of farsightedness. Just before his inauguration, Bill Clinton reflected on his accomplishments as governor of Arkansas. His proudest achievement, he said, was to teach the people of Arkansas to think long term. "It's what I most want to do nationwide. It won't be easy and it will require constant dialogue with the country. But it has to be done and I mean to do it."

Deficit reduction moved to the top of America's public agenda in February 1993 when President Clinton laid out his economic plan. In a major speech to Congress that took the debt problem seriously, Clinton underscored his intention to encourage the nation to think long term. He described the kinds of sacrifices that will be necessary to reduce the deficit over the next few years. Clinton proposed a comprehensive program of tax increases and spending cuts designed to trim the federal budget over the next four years by more than $300 billion.

The question now is not only whether Congress chooses to follow that prescription but what the American public thinks of it, and whether there is broad support for the kinds of measures the president is proposing. Because any realistic deficit-reduction plan will involve sacrifices, the public has to be convinced that it is a matter of some urgency to deal with the debt problem. And the public must be involved in decisions about how those sacrifices will be shared.

Commentator David Gergen recently remarked that "America is at a hinge point in history that demands new thinking — and a new consensus — if we are to shape a congenial life for the next generation." It is hard to imagine that the life of future generations will be very congenial if the public debt climbs to a projected level of almost $6 trillion by the turn of the century.

Our purpose in this issue book, and in nationwide Forums on the debt, is to stimulate public deliberation about what is widely regarded as the nation's most pressing problem and work toward common ground on which to assemble an acceptable package of deficit-reducing measures.

Keith Melville, Managing Editor

Managing Editor: Keith Melville
Writers: Keith Melville, Bill Carr
Boxed Features: Bill Carr
Research: Bill Carr
Editor: Betty Frecker
Ballots: Randa Slim, Steve Farkas, Ilse Tebbetts
Graphic Research: Bill Carr

Production Manager: George Cavanaugh
Designer: Sundberg & Associates Inc
Circulation Coordinator: Victoria Simpson
Cover Illustration: David Gothard
Formatting: Parker Advertising
Production Director: Robert E. Daley

The books in this series are prepared jointly by the Public Agenda Foundation — a nonprofit, nonpartisan organization devoted to research and education about public issues — and by the Kettering Foundation. The Kendall/ Hunt Publishing Company prints and distributes these books. They are used by civic and educational organizations interested in addressing public issues.

In particular, they are used in local discussion groups that are part of a nationwide network, the National Issues Forums (NIF). The NIF consists of more than 4,000 civic and educational organizations — colleges and universities, libraries, service clubs, and membership groups. Although each community group is locally controlled, NIF is a collaborative effort. Each year, convenors choose three issues and use common materials — issue books such as this one, and parallel audio and videotape materials.

Groups interested in using the NIF materials and adapting its approach as part of their own program are invited to write or call for further information: National Issues Forums, 100 Commons Road, Dayton, Ohio 45459-2777. Phone 1-800-433-7834.

The NIF issue books — both the standard edition and an abridged version at a lower reading level, as well as audiocassette and videocassette versions of the same material — can be ordered from Kendall/Hunt Publishing Company, 2460 Kerper Boulevard, Dubuque, Iowa 52004-0539. Phone 1-800-228-0810. The following titles are available:

The $4 Trillion Debt: Tough Choices about Soaring Federal Deficits
The Poverty Puzzle: What Should Be Done to Help the Poor?
Prescription for Prosperity: Four Paths to Economic Renewal
Criminal Violence: What Direction Now for the War on Crime?
People and Politics: Who Should Govern?
Education: How Do We Get the Results We Want?
The Health Care Crisis: Containing Costs, Expanding Coverage
The Boundaries of Free Speech: How Free Is Too Free?
America's Role in the World: New Risks, New Realities
Energy Options: Finding a Solution to the Power Predicament
The Battle over Abortion: Seeking Common Ground in a Divided Nation
Regaining the Competitive Edge: Are We Up to the Job?
Remedies for Racial Inequality: Why Progress Has Stalled, What Should Be Done
The Day Care Dilemma: Who Should Be Responsible for the Children?
The Drug Crisis: Public Strategies for Breaking the Habit
The Environment at Risk: Responding to Growing Dangers
Health Care for the Elderly: Moral Dilemmas, Mortal Choices
Coping with AIDS: The Public Response to the Epidemic

300 B

DAVID GOTHARD

THE $4 TRILLION DEBT:
TOUGH CHOICES ABOUT SOARING FEDERAL DEFICITS

PREPARED BY THE PUBLIC AGENDA FOUNDATION

CONTENTS

SEA OF RED INK:
LIVING BEYOND OUR MEANS

"While citizens and elected officials repeatedly affirm their commitment to a balanced budget, the gap between government spending and revenues grows wider. The question is whether we can find a way to kick the debt habit."

In his 1992 campaign manifesto, *United We Stand*, H. Ross Perot addressed one of the central themes of his candidacy, the national debt and the failure of one president after another to address it, or do anything about it. The national debt, said Perot with his characteristic candor, "is like a crazy aunt we keep down in the basement. All the neighbors know she's there, but nobody wants to talk about her."

The events of 1992 offered ample evidence that the problem has been getting worse. During fiscal year 1992, the federal government spent $5 for every $4 it collected in revenues and borrowed the difference. By September 30, the end of the government's fiscal year, the deficit reached a record $290 billion.

Public deficits are likely to soar to even higher levels over the next few years. In a report released in January 1993, the Congressional Budget Office (CBO) estimated that if federal spending and tax policies remain unchanged, the deficit will reach $650 billion by fiscal year 2003 and the debt will be roughly $7.5 trillion. Quite simply, says Joseph Minarik, chief economist for the Office of Management and Budget, "the deficit is on an unsustainable path."

Judging by recent opinion polls, the public doesn't need to be convinced of the need to close the budget gap. When the Times Mirror Center for the People and the Press polled voters just before the 1992 election, deficit reduction was named most frequently as the top priority for the next president. "It was unbelievable to us," said Andrew Kohut, who directed the survey. "The deficit got more first place mentions than the economy and jobs. We haven't seen these kinds of numbers before with the deficit."

Leaders are also concerned about the problem. In October 1992, the Strengthening of America Commission, a bipartisan group of business leaders and elected officials, issued a report urging immediate action to reduce federal deficits by a total of $2 trillion by the year 2002. In their introduction to the report, Senators Sam Nunn and Pete Domenici, who chaired the commission, underlined the importance of prompt action. "We believe it is time for leaders to talk frankly to the American people about the seriousness of our present situation and about the sacrifices and hard choices we must make now if we want to put our economy on the path toward long-term economic growth."

PAINFUL SOLUTIONS

However important it is to talk frankly about the deficit, the 1992 presidential election demonstrated that mainstream politicians will do almost anything to avoid the topic. Any realistic solution for reducing the deficit promises to be painful. Presidential candidates who have talked candidly about what needs to be done to tame the deficit — including Walter Mondale in 1984, Robert Dole in 1988, and Paul Tsongas in 1992 — have paid a price for doing so.

During the presidential campaign, President Bush and Bill Clinton were notably reluctant to utter the dreaded D-word. In his 1992 State of the Union address, President Bush mentioned the deficit only once. During the campaign, Bush referred to mild deficit-reduction measures, and for the most part, unrealistic ones. He offered few specifics about how such measures might be implemented. In one proposal, Bush proposed putting a cap on mandatory spending programs such as Medicare. But he did not say where the line should be drawn or whose benefits would be affected. Far from suggesting that tax increases might be necessary to control soaring deficits, President Bush dangled the prospect of tax *reductions* throughout the campaign. Like those miracle "eat-all-you-want-and-*still*-lose-weight diets" that are advertised on television, President Bush implied that the deficit could be reduced without pain or sacrifice.

For his part, Governor Clinton also treated the deficit issue gingerly during the campaign. Although he promised to cut the deficit in half in four years, Clinton didn't do much better than President Bush when it came to offering realistic proposals for achieving that goal. Clinton proposed further cuts in military spending and tax hikes for the wealthiest Americans. But at the same time, he held out the prospect of reduced taxes for middle-class families. On various occasions, Clinton said that federal revenues could be raised by $45 billion if tax laws that apply to foreign companies operating in the United States were enforced, an assertion that many experts questioned.

Only when independent candidate Ross Perot tossed his hat into the ring was there a candidate willing to call attention to the deficit. As a plain-spoken outsider, Perot said what the others could not say, that just about everyone is to blame for the $4 trillion debt. If we are serious about reducing the deficit, said Perot, we need to consider spending cuts in many areas, as well as tax increases.

In February 1993, less than 30 days after he took office, President Clinton laid out, in an economic address to Congress, what he intends to do about the deficit. Warning that the nation "risks losing the standard of living it has taken for granted" if it does not take a new economic course, Clinton proposed a comprehensive package of measures intended to reduce the budget gap.

He proposed terminating or reducing spending on more than 150 federal projects, ranging from the space station to agricultural subsidies, as well as deeper defense cuts than those previously announced. And he proposed a series of new taxes designed to raise $246 billion in additional revenues over the next four years.

"For years," said Clinton, "there has

been a lot of talk about the deficit, but very few credible efforts to deal with it. This plan tackles the deficit seriously and over the long term."

With the announcement of his deficit-reduction plan, President Clinton opened a new round of debate and public discussion about a problem that elected officials have, for the most part, tried to avoid. Whether the public supports the Clinton plan, or other deficit-reduction proposals, depends in large part on whether most Americans agree that bitter medicine is needed to deal with a serious problem.

A BINGE OF BORROWING

If the government spends $1.4 trillion during the year but takes in just $1.1 trillion, as it did in fiscal year 1992, it must borrow the difference, some $290 billion. Each year the government runs in the red, the amount it borrows is added to deficits from preceding years.

The total figure is the federal debt, which in 1992 passed the $4 trillion mark.

Living on credit is an alluring habit. Ask any of the 110 million Americans who hold credit cards — on average, eight cards apiece. Spending on credit appeals to elected officials for the same reasons it appeals to individuals. Borrowing permits elected officials to support new (and politically popular) spending programs, while avoiding the (politically unpopular) taxes that would otherwise be needed to pay for them. For a while, at least, the illusion of seeming wealthier than you actually are can be sustained.

Eventually, however, interest payments on outstanding debt become a heavy burden. Just as individuals must pay interest on unpaid loans or credit card charges, the federal government is obliged to pay interest on the money it borrows. As each year's deficit is added to accumulated debt from previous years, an increasing portion of the taxes we pay must be set aside for interest payments. In 1992, interest payments by the federal government came to about $200 billion, which is roughly 14 percent of all federal spending.

Deficit spending is nothing new. Between 1789 and 1930, the amount spent by the federal government exceeded the amount it collected in revenues about one in every three years. In particular, government has often borrowed to cover military spending during wartime.

The habit of deficit spending has grown worse in recent years. During the eight years of the Reagan administration, the country engaged in what former Federal Reserve Board Chairman Paul Volcker called "a national binge of borrowing." Over that period, the federal debt grew by $1.3 trillion. Today's taxpayers are picking up the bill for that binge. This year, next year, and the year after that, taxpayers will be obliged to pay more than $65 billion annually to cover interest charges on debt accumulated during the Reagan years alone.

DRAINING DEFICITS

Some economists remain unconvinced that public indebtedness at current levels is a serious problem. Despite large deficits, interests rates are still low, inflation remains at a manageable level, and foreign investors are still willing to lend us money. Most economists, however, are concerned about growing indebtedness. Many are convinced that the nation is already paying a high price for living beyond our means. A 1993 CBO report showed that the federal debt amounts to more than half of the nation's Gross Domestic Product (the total output of goods and services), up from 26 percent in 1981.

From month to month, the effects of deficit spending are hard to detect. Charles Schultze, who served as chairman of President Carter's Council of Economic Advisors, compared the deficit to termites in the basement. Rather than posing an imminent threat, government borrowing gradually erodes our economic strength by undermining the foundation.

Experts acknowledge that the deficit isn't the only cause of America's economic troubles. But, says Harvard economist Benjamin Friedman, "the deficit has been the greatest single force underlying the most severe failures of America's economic performance since the 1980s, especially those with the most troubling implications for the future."

Huge public deficits create a drag on the economy in three respects:

• *Large deficits absorb savings that would otherwise be available for private investment.* When the U.S. Treasury borrows, it takes money that could be used by private investors to build housing, expand factories, and develop new technologies. Currently, the federal government borrows an amount equivalent to almost all of the private savings in the United States.

• *Large deficits drive up interest rates, which make it harder for consumers to borrow money and for entrepreneurs to start new enterprises.* To cover its debt, the government competes with other borrowers, such as individuals who seek mortgages for new homes, or entrepreneurs who want to expand their businesses. This competition drives up

HOW DEFICIT SPENDING AFFECTS YOU

• Divided among 256 million U.S. citizens, the $4 trillion debt comes to $15,625 for every man, woman, and child. That's $62,500 for a family of four.
• At the current rate of deficit spending, the national debt is growing at the mind-boggling rate of $40 million an hour, or $1 billion a day. To cover the wide gap between spending and revenues, the federal government is forced to borrow $1,200 per year for every person in the United States.
• Experts estimate that, as a result of the huge increase in government debt over the past decade, interest rates are one to three percentage points higher than they would otherwise be. Higher interest rates make it harder for individuals and businesses to afford loans to buy homes or start new enterprises.
• In 1992, interest payments on the federal debt cost taxpayers $199 billion. Since there are about 115 million taxpayers, that comes to $1,730 for a typical taxpayer. Because individuals pay taxes over a period of 50 years or so, your portion of the bill for interest on the debt is roughly $86,500 (and this figure is based on the unlikely supposition that the debt will not continue to grow).
• A recent report from the Federal Reserve Bank concluded that because deficits soared in the 1980s, the U.S. economy produces about $210 billion less in goods and services than it would have if deficits had remained at their former level. That translates into a reduction in the standard of living of every U.S. citizen of more than $800 per year.

> "We need to find a fair way to share the pain that will accompany any realistic plan to close the awesome gap between the cost of public programs and the government's revenues."

interest rates, which makes it more difficult for individuals and businesses to afford loans.

• *Large deficits increase our dependence on foreign lenders.* Foreign investors, who own about 20 percent of U.S. Treasury bonds, play an important role in supporting the habit of deficit spending. As foreign investors control ever-larger amounts of the federal debt, they can impose tougher terms, or cut off their credit.

A huge public debt has other corrosive effects. Because the federal government spends almost $200 billion a year on interest payments, those funds are unavailable for other purposes such as improving the schools, dealing with the drug problem, or funding research and development to keep American industry competitive.

The habit of deficit spending also violates the moral compact between the generations, and it undermines the country's future prosperity. As Friedman writes in *Day of Reckoning*, the belief that men and women should strive to create a better future for their children is "the basic moral principle that has bound each generation of Americans to the next since the founding of the Republic." However, Friedman says, "Since 1980, we have broken with that tradition by pursuing a policy that amounts to living not just in but for the present. America has thrown itself a party and billed the tab to the future."

That is why many people are convinced that the habit of deficit spending must be curbed. "Adopting a different economic policy," says Friedman, "is not just an economic matter but a moral imperative. If we do not correct America's fiscal course, our children and our children's children will have the right to hold us responsible."

HARD CHOICES

Why is the habit of living beyond our means so hard to break? On a day-to-day basis, elected officials are under far more pressure to say yes to spending proposals than they are to say no. They are also under pressure

not to raise taxes. By running deficits, members of Congress can satisfy the demands of particular interest groups and reap the political benefits of doing so, without antagonizing the public by raising taxes.

In the words of James R. Jones, former chairman of the House Budget Committee, "The biggest problem in reforming the system is that there is no pressure on Congress to make hard choices. The missing ingredient is public pressure to solve the deficit problem."

The task of public forums on deficit reduction is to examine various proposals, especially the deficit-reduction package put forward by President Clinton in February. The goal is to see if we can agree on a variety of measures that are broadly acceptable to the American public.

To reduce a budget gap that is projected to be more than $300 billion in 1993, we need to look at the entire range of alternatives for reducing government spending and raising revenues. In the words of Joseph Minarik, "You can't come up with $200 billion or

NICULAE ASCIU

more per year without touching virtually every section of the federal government. There's no question it will be painful." Because almost everyone will be affected by the measures necessary to reduce the deficit, public participation in the debate is essential.

In this issue book, we examine four

options for reducing the deficit. The choices the nation faces are similar to the options available to individuals when personal expenses exceed their income. We can scale back or eliminate certain expenditures. Or we can raise our income. It is a question of principles and priorities: How much government do we want, for what purposes? And how much are we willing to pay for it?

Choice #1 proposes to trim the budget by reducing discretionary spending, a catchall category for what Congress spends each year on a wide array of services and programs, including national parks, medical research, aid to education, and disaster relief.

Choice #2 proposes to close the budget gap by cutting the defense budget. To decide which expenditures are necessary, we need to reexamine America's global role and ask which military commitments we are prepared to scale down.

Choice #3 proposes to trim the budget by scaling down entitlement programs. This large and rapidly growing portion of the federal budget includes the Social Security program, Medicare, Medicaid, and farm price-support programs.

Choice #4 proposes to reduce the deficit by raising federal revenues. Options include tax hikes on upper-income taxpayers, increasing special taxes, such as the gas tax or tobacco taxes, and imposing a federal consumption tax.

Since the gap between federal spending and revenues is so large, it is generally agreed that some combination of these measures will be necessary. It is not enough to rail against huge deficits, or to blame elected officials for their repeated failure to balance the budget. We, the American public, need to examine these deficit-reduction options and decide which measures we are prepared to accept. Most important, we need to decide on a fair way to share the pain that will accompany any realistic plan for reducing the federal deficit.■

CHOICE #1
DISCRETIONARY SPENDING:
A GUIDED TOUR OF FEDERAL PROGRAMS

"Reducing discretionary spending is one way to close the budget gap. Choosing among government programs and benefits forces us to decide on our priorities, and make some tough choices about what we're prepared to give up."

In 1992, the sprawling enterprise called the federal government spent a grand total of almost $1.4 trillion. To examine what your tax dollars buy, open the pages of the annual *Budget of the United States Government*, a hefty volume larger than the Manhattan phone book, which lists government spending programs and their cost.

Despite the profusion of detail about how much the federal government spends on thousands of different agencies and programs, one thing you will notice is that most federal spending goes for just three categories. For each dollar the government spent in 1992:

• *Fourteen cents, or roughly $200 billion, paid for interest on the $4 trillion national debt.* Since this figure represents the outstanding debt for all federal borrowing, it cannot be reduced.

• *Forty-nine cents, or some $711 billion, paid for direct benefits to individuals, called entitlements.* This category includes benefits paid through Social Security, Medicare, Medicaid, unemployment benefits, and federal employee and veterans' pensions.

• *Twenty-one cents, or $304 billion, paid for national defense,* including three million civilian and military personnel; the cost of purchasing, maintaining, and upgrading weapons systems; and the cost of a worldwide network of military bases.

That leaves about 16 cents, or $233 billion, for a catchall category called discretionary spending. This category includes all of the other federal projects, agencies, programs, and services. These include the FBI, national parks, space exploration, medical research, drug abuse prevention, foreign aid, disaster relief, highway construction, and aid to handicapped children. This is also the part of the budget that covers the salaries of all nondefense federal employees, including the president and members of Congress.

The problem, as advocates of a first perspective on deficit reduction see it, is that the federal government is too big and too costly. Both the size and cost of the federal government have grown dramatically over the past half century. The Congressional Budget Office reports that federal spending in 1993 will approach 25 percent of Gross Domestic Product (GDP), a postwar high.

It is time to recognize, in Ross Perot's words, that "government is not a candy store in which every group can pick from any jar it wants. This is not free money. It's your money. More importantly, it's your children's money. It is time to adjust our spending to what

GENE BASSET

we can afford."

Judging from recent polls, a majority of the American public feels that federal spending is excessive and that taxpayers don't get their money's worth. In the words of columnist Donald Lambro, "Lawmakers have created a costly labyrinth of inefficient, overlapping, and nonessential agencies and programs that squander our tax dollars. The budget is still loaded with programs and agencies whose elimination would harm no one. Tens of billions of dollars in potential savings could be used to reduce the deficit."

WHAT SHOULD BE CUT?

While many people agree that the government is bloated, there is little agreement about which discretionary programs should be cut.

On the eve of the Clinton inaugural, columnist Lars-Erik Nelson assembled a list of "very expensive things we can do without." Nelson's list began with the U.S. Department of Agriculture, which he describes as "100,000 bureaucrats distributing benefits to 300,000 farmers." Nelson also wants to eliminate the National Endowment for the Arts, a federal agency that received $175 million in 1992. In Nelson's view, the NEA "hands out money, not necessarily to artists, but certainly to artsy-seeming people who know how to get grants from government bureaucracies."

No two people are likely to agree about which programs are essential and which should be eliminated. However, most advocates of reducing discretionary spending agree on several principles. Senator Pete Domenici proposes two tests for deciding what should be eliminated. If the program did not already exist, would Congress fund it and would the public support it? Is the program or activity a federal responsibility, or could it be carried out in the private sector? Most advocates of this choice would agree on a third criterion. Is the program a luxury item, something the nation may have been able to afford when the economy was growing rapidly

THE FEDERAL SPENDING DOLLAR, 1992

49¢ **DIRECT BENEFIT PAYMENTS TO INDIVIDUALS**　21¢ **NATIONAL DEFENSE**　16¢ **DISCRETIONARY SPENDING**　14¢ **INTEREST ON THE NATIONAL DEBT**

Congressional Budget Office, January 1993

in the 1960s, but cannot afford any longer?

If you examine the spending programs in the federal budget, you will find various items that cannot be justified in light of the nation's current needs and problems. Consider, for example, subsidies to encourage production of wool, which were put into effect when wool was needed for military uniforms. Though synthetic materials have long since knocked wool off the list of strategic goods, many farmers still receive government subsidies through this program, which costs taxpayers $180 million a year.

Another case in point is the U.S. Information Agency and the Voice of America. During World War II and the Cold War, these agencies — which beamed American broadcasts to listeners behind the Iron Curtain — made sense. But circumstances have changed. Communism no longer poses a threat to us. And advances in communication technology have overtaken shortwave radio broadcasts. As Lars-Erik Nelson notes, "These agencies have been superceded by CNN and MTV, which bring American news and culture in living color to TV sets around the world. Broadcasting government propaganda by shortwave is obsolete."

As a first order of business, say proponents of this choice, it is essential to review all federal programs regularly, and eliminate those that are no

longer needed.

Proponents of this choice also favor the elimination of federal activities that could be performed by private sector firms. Over the past decade, privatization of public services has been a worldwide trend. Nations ranging from Australia to Argentina have sold state-owned programs and activities to private corporations. Advocates of this choice believe the United States would do well to follow the lead of other nations in this regard.

One example of a public agency that could be privatized, say advocates, is the U.S. Postal Service. In the words of former Budget Director James C. Miller, "It is time to end the postal service's monopoly over the mails. Several think tanks have documented that greater use of private sector alternatives would produce savings and improve the quality of service. What do we have to lose by allowing private companies to compete with the postal service?"

A third category of government spending projects that should be eliminated, say advocates of this choice, are those that could be considered luxuries. Advocates of this choice agree with the Strengthening of America Commission that, at a time when the federal government runs huge deficits, "there are a number of areas in which federal spending cannot be justified."

One item on the "luxury" list is the space station. One of the most controversial projects administered by the National Aeronautics and Space Administration, the space station is projected to cost almost $20 billion over the next ten years. Congress has instructed NASA to scale down spending for the space station by 15 percent. But many people are convinced that the project should be terminated. "I'm a supporter of scientific research," says

Ross Perot. "However, this is a huge undertaking for a nation with a deficit of almost $300 billion. We should defer the space station until we have the money to pay for it."

Spending could be reduced in a less selective way, by making across-the-board cuts in all discretionary programs. Many of those who favor reducing the deficit by cutting discretionary spending support measures such as the Gramm-Rudman-Hollings Act of 1987, which was superceded by the Budget Enforcement Act of 1990. The act mandates that if the deficit is not reduced each year by a certain amount, automatic across-the-board spending cuts go into effect.

During the presidential campaign, Ross Perot proposed a 10 percent across-the-board cut in discretionary spending, which he said would result in savings of $108 billion over five years.

We need to acknowledge, say advocates of this choice, that although the United States is a rich nation, it is not rich enough to permit all the government activities we might want. To live within our means, we have to ask which programs are essential and what we can do without. The bottom line, in the words of columnist Thomas Sowell, is that "If you are not prepared to curb spending, you can forget about reducing the national debt."

WHAT CRITICS SAY

To critics, trying to close the budget gap by slashing discretionary spending is both unrealistic and unwise. It is easy to find certain activities that seem less than essential. But it is inaccurate to say that most federal spending for discretionary programs is frittered away.

While critics concede that some pork barrel spending projects can still be found, they point out that there is a lot less "pork" in the budget than there used to be. In the words of *Washington Post* reporter Paul Blustein, "Nearly all the parts of the budget that tend to be porky shrank substantially during the 1980s."

Artist's rendering of the NASA space station: An essential program or an unaffordable luxury?

It is inaccurate, say critics, to say that most federal spending is wasted on unnecessary programs. To the contrary, this small portion of the federal budget pays for a variety of programs on which the American public depends. With these funds, government runs the national parks, regulates environmental pollution, builds highways and bridges, arrests drug traffickers, and provides a wide range of social services. Nearly half of the discretionary spending budget is used for social programs such as education, income security, and health care (not including the Medicare and Medicaid programs).

After a decade in which discretionary spending has been repeatedly cut back, say critics, it is important to acknowledge that certain public needs cannot be deferred any longer. "In its efforts to hold down the budget," says Charles Schultze, "Congress has penny-pinched virtually all civilian programs aside from Social Security — the necessary along with the wasteful. Consequently, agencies such as the Bureau of Prisons, the Coast Guard, and the National Science Foundation have accumulated a backlog of unmet needs."

Critics also insist that, in most cases, government activities cannot be performed as cheaply or as well by the private sector. Defending the U.S. Postal Service, Moe Biller, president of the American Postal Workers Union, says, "The privatization peddlers preach that

America's postal service needs a healthy dose of competition. They dream of dozens, perhaps hundreds of private postal companies, outdoing one another. It would be chaos."

Critics are particularly concerned about the effects of further cutbacks in public investments such as highways, bridges, and other public works. President Clinton has pointed out on various occasions that the United States has "an investment deficit as well as a budget deficit." Far from agreeing with advocates of trimming public spending, critics believe that the government should *increase* spending in this area. When properly targeted, critics assert, investment spending spurs economic growth. By generating additional public revenues, a growing economy helps to reduce the deficit.

Critics object especially to proposals for across-the-board cuts in discretionary spending. Cutting the deficit by reducing most spending programs by the same percentage is both mindless and harmful. Across-the-board cuts, they contend, would lead to senseless reductions in essential public programs, such as federal aid to education and health programs for women and children.

There is a final reason, say critics, why this is not a promising way to balance the budget. Compared to other parts of the budget, none of the discretionary spending programs carries a big price tag. In his 1993 budget, George Bush proposed to cut 246 federal programs. The proposal sounded like a substantial step toward reducing the deficit. But even if Mr. Bush had succeeded in making every one of those cuts — most of which were to come out of discretionary spending — it would have saved just $5 billion, which is less than 2 percent of what is needed to cover the projected 1993 deficit.

Many people believe that there is a good deal more fat in the defense budget, and that is where spending cuts should be made. So let us examine the argument for reducing the deficit by paring down defense spending.■

CHOICE #2
DEFENSE DECISIONS:
HOW MUCH MORE CAN BE CUT?

"The United States faces fundamental decisions about its role in the world, and what kind of military we need under dramatically changed circumstances. At a time of growing pressure to cut spending, how much more can be cut from the defense budget?"

In 1992, $304 billion, or 21 cents out of every federal dollar, went for defense. Because the United States spends so much on defense and because of the "peace dividend" that was promised at the end of the Cold War, the military budget has figured prominently in recent discussions about how to reduce the deficit.

Throughout the Cold War era, the prospect of military confrontation with the Soviet Union and its allies was the threat that determined the size and shape of the U.S. armed forces. As leader of the free world and chief defender against Soviet expansionism, the United States invested $12 trillion (in 1992 dollars) over a period of 45 years in national defense.

The end of the Cold War dramatically altered the international scene. Because of it, direct threats to the United States, its allies, and its interests have rapidly subsided. Acknowledging those rapid changes, Congress and the president agreed, in the 1990 budget summit, to reduce the defense budget 20 percent by 1995. In 1991, after the dissolution of the Soviet Union, President Bush proposed an additional $50 billion in reductions, which would trim defense spending 25 percent by 1997.

Those cuts, which reflect

the Pentagon's assessment of the "base force" this country needs in the post-Cold War era, are now under way. By 1993, the Department of Defense was about halfway toward its goal of reducing military forces by 400,000. Plans are also under way to reduce the number of U.S. troops in Europe by about half, and to close many military bases both at home and abroad. In April 1992, the Pentagon reported that about 500 sites worldwide had been trimmed or shut down. By 1995, the U.S. will have reduced overseas military sites by about 40 percent. The Congressional Budget Office (CBO) estimates that the "peace dividend" will consist of annual savings of as much as $100 billion a year by 1997.

But advocates of this choice are convinced that even more should be cut from the defense budget. Soon after Bill Clinton took office in 1993, he an-

DICK WALLMEYER/LONG BEACH PRESS TELEGRAM

nounced additional cuts of $11 billion a year in defense spending. Commenting on that announcement, the editors of *USA Today* noted that defense spending at the level proposed by the new administration is in line with President Clinton's campaign pledge to reduce Pentagon spending by $60 billion over 5 years. But they also noted that that figure is "more than the country needs to spend in the post-Cold War world. The suspicion lingers that the military, aided by a pork barreling Congress, is a little too good at defending itself from one thing: the deficit-cutting knife."

Proponents of this choice are convinced that there is a strong argument for deeper defense cuts than those anticipated in the Pentagon's "base force" plan or those favored by President Clinton. In the words of Jack Beatty, senior editor at *The Atlantic*, "The main threats to our international position are domestic. They are to be found in the debt-ridden condition of our economy and the deteriorating state of much of our physical and human capital. This is the realm in which we will be tested in the post-Cold War era. We have a choice between Cold War and post-Cold War ideas of strength, between yesterday and tomorrow."

Advocates of this choice acknowledge the importance of military preparedness to deal with such dangers as terrorism, drug trafficking, and nuclear proliferation. In the words of Peter Peterson, investment banker and cofounder of the Concord Coalition, an organization that is generating support for deficit reduction, "We still have external threats and obviously we must be prepared to meet them." But Peterson believes that "we can meet our security needs with a defense budget substantially smaller than the one we have now."

In discussions on Capitol Hill about how much farther the defense budget can be reduced, William Kaufmann and John Steinbruner, authors of a recent report from the Brookings Institution entitled *Decisions for Defense*, have made the case for cutting defense spending 50 percent by the year 2001, which would save billions of dollars more than the Pentagon's "base force" plan. Even if the defense budget is cut by 50 percent, they argue, the Pentagon could maintain "high readiness, rapid overseas deployment, and continued modernization through the upgrading of current weapons systems."

MISSION CONTROL

Among people familiar with military hardware, debate about defense spending often consists of comparing lists of which weapons should be eliminated, and how much could be saved by doing so.

Before deciding which military tools are needed, we need to ask a series of questions about the job America's armed forces are expected to perform. To answer these questions, we need to reexamine the mission of the U.S. military in light of the new realities of the post-Cold War period.

Throughout the Cold War, most of the U.S. military budget was used to finance three missions. The first mission was to maintain the capacity to deter a nuclear attack, and if necessary fight a nuclear war. To fulfill this objective, the Department of Defense developed a huge arsenal of strategic weapons, including bombers equipped with nuclear warheads and an array of land-based and submarine-based missiles.

The second mission was to help America's allies in the North Atlantic Treaty Organization (NATO) defend Western Europe against attack by the Soviet-led Warsaw Pact nations. To guard against such an attack, 350,000 American troops were stationed in Europe as recently as the mid-1980s, along with a substantial number of tanks, aircraft, and other combat weapons.

The third mission of the U.S. military was to be prepared to deploy American military forces to several regions of the world at the same time. To protect America's allies and interests worldwide, the Pentagon maintained airlift and sealift capabilities, and it maintained 100 military bases overseas. In pursuit of these three missions, by the late 1980s the U.S. military was spending more than $1,000 per year for every man, woman, and child in the United States.

Proponents of a 50 percent cut in defense spending insist that it is time to redefine these missions. In the post-Cold War period, they argue, the defense budget could be trimmed substantially without threatening our national security.

With regard to the first mission, proponents argue that we no longer need a huge nuclear arsenal. Since the Soviet threat has diminished, it makes sense to sharply reduce spending on strategic arms. And, proponents point out, the situation in Europe has changed fundamentally. As Ross Perot writes in *United We Stand,* "We cannot justify using U.S. taxpayers' money to protect Western Europe from potential intra-European strife. The Europeans — thanks in part to our presence for the past 45 years — have the ability to do this for themselves."

To proponents of sharp cuts in the defense budget, the U.S. military commitment in Europe is a symbol of a larger problem, our habit of maintaining a worldwide military presence. Given the urgent need to balance the budget, advocates of defense cuts assert that the United States can no longer afford such a far-reaching military presence. Even some former Pentagon officials acknowledge this necessity. As former Navy Secretary John Lehman says, "We have to stop living beyond our means and playing as if we can be the world's policeman."

As advocates of this position see it, we should seek collective security and burden sharing— an arrangement in which each nation contributes forces and financial resources to multinational peacekeeping efforts.

In the words of columnist David Gergen, "Collective leadership is the order of the day. For a nation long accustomed to giving out orders, it won't be easy to live with diminished power, but we have no choice."

WHAT CRITICS SAY

Critics differ sharply in their assessment of the world situation, their view of the role America should play in the post-Cold War era, and whether it is wise to cut the defense budget beyond the reductions described in the Pentagon's "base force" plan.

Critics contend that, while the threat of superpower confrontation has sharply diminished, new global realities are both threatening and unstable. Given the instabilities that exist in the new world order, critics say, it would be premature to scale down America's global role.

It is worth recalling, say advocates of a strong defense, that the first year of

the post-Cold War era brought not just Iraq's invasion of Kuwait, but also heightened conflict between Israel and its Arab neighbors, violent civil war in Liberia, and tensions between India and Pakistan that almost erupted into war.

And European security is still an issue. While the Soviet Union has dissolved, it left behind an immense arsenal of military hardware and trained military personnel in Europe. As demonstrated by the war in Yugoslavia, violent eruptions among the newly independent states of the former Soviet Union are still entirely possible.

Considering the harsh realities of the post-Cold War era, say critics of defense cuts, the United States has no

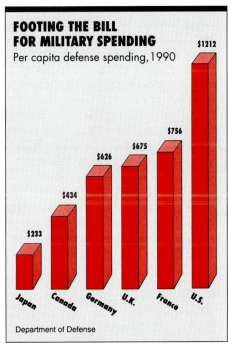

FOOTING THE BILL FOR MILITARY SPENDING
Per capita defense spending, 1990

- Japan $233
- Canada $434
- Germany $626
- U.K. $675
- France $756
- U.S. $1212

Department of Defense

choice but to take a leading role. As former Assistant Secretary of State Elliott Abrams puts it, "American leadership is a precondition for a peaceful world." As desirable as it may be to share the peace-keeping burden with other nations, it is difficult to arrange multinational coalitions in times of crisis. In situations that call for immediate action, say critics, the United States must be prepared to act alone.

Critics caution against making deeper cuts than those called for in the Pentagon's "base force" plan. As they see it, there is no such thing as being a superpower on the cheap. If deeper cuts in the defense budget are made, the United States may end up with the same kind of "hollow force" it had in the late 1970s, when sharp cutbacks undermined the ability of the armed forces to respond effectively to crises.

Critics point to another reason why further cuts in the defense budget are ill advised. As a result of military downsizing, more than 300,000 jobs have been lost in defense-related industries. Since the "base force" plan calls for additional spending reductions, further job losses are bound to take place. At a time when joblessness is already a major concern, we can hardly afford to add to the ranks of the unemployed.

There is one final reason to look for other solutions to the budget crisis, no matter what is done about the defense budget. To many Americans, deep cuts in defense are the preferred solution to the budget crisis. They imagine that, if such cuts are made, painful measures such as raising taxes or scaling down federal entitlements would be unnecessary.

But that is unrealistic for two reasons. First, substantial cuts in the defense budget have already been factored into deficit projections. Before he left office, President Bush called for defense cuts that would reduce military spending by 25 percent by 1997. Even with those cuts, deficits are expected to be unacceptably high. At some point, spending reductions will have to come from other parts of the budget. And second, even if the Pentagon were closed, all 4 of the armed services disbanded, and 3 million Pentagon employees worldwide given pink slips, the amount saved — some $300 billion — would not be enough to cover the projected deficit for 1993.

Let us turn to the portion of the budget that covers entitlement spending, a large and rapidly growing fraction of the federal budget.■

CHOICE #3
THE UNCONTROLLABLES:
PUTTING A LID ON ENTITLEMENTS

"A large and rapidly growing portion of federal spending goes for cash payments to individuals. While many agree that entitlement spending needs to be controlled, there is little agreement about how to do so."

In a famous exchange, notorious criminal Willie Sutton was once asked why he robbed banks. Without skipping a beat, he replied, "Because that's where the money is." For the same reason, many are convinced that, if we're serious about reducing the deficit, something has to be done about the entitlement programs. In 1992, roughly half of all federal spending covered benefits to individuals through entitlement programs such as Social Security, Medicare, farm price supports, veterans' pensions and unemployment compensation.

Government programs that provide benefits to individuals — in the form of cash or non-cash assistance — are called "entitlements" because citizens who meet certain qualifications are automatically entitled to receive them. The enactment of the Social Security program was one of the first steps to establish a system of federal benefits to individuals, and it remains by far the largest. Since the 1930s, other entitlement programs have been established. Some — such as food stamps and Medicaid — provide benefits to people with low incomes. But most entitlement spending, about four-fifths of it, goes for programs that are provided to individuals who qualify regardless of income level.

No matter how difficult it is to trim programs that provide benefits to millions of Americans, advocates of this third choice are convinced that it is necessary to do so. "For anyone who imagines curbing the budget deficit," writes *New York Times* reporter Erik Eckholm, "the huge, mostly tax-free benefits that flow to the elderly, mainly via Social Security and Medicare, present unavoidable targets — money monsters that must be tamed. If, as many economists think, the deficit should be Public Issue Number 1, these soaring payments should be Topic A."

THEY KEEP GROWING

Entitlement programs are different from discretionary programs in two important respects. Unlike other spending programs, Congress does not review spending on entitlements as part of its annual budgeting process. And unlike discretionary programs, no one knows for sure how much entitlements will cost from year to year. When Congress allots a certain amount for a highway project, for instance, no more than that amount can

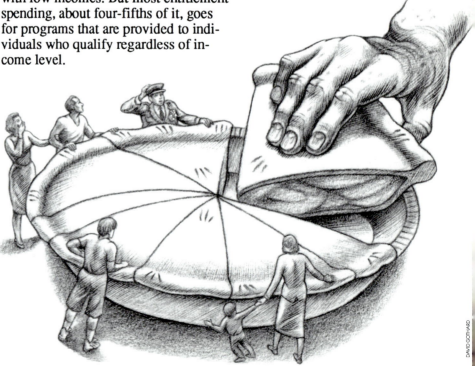

DAVID GOTHARD

legally be spent. But because entitlement benefits are issued to anyone who is eligible, no one knows how many people will qualify — and how much the programs will cost.

That's the problem, say advocates of this choice. The cost of entitlement programs just keeps growing, regardless of the nation's ability to afford them. Not all of the entitlement programs are expanding rapidly. The cost of the Food Stamp program, for example, is projected to rise only slightly over the next 5 years, from its current level of $23 billion. The problem lies in the three largest and most rapidly growing entitlement programs: Social Security, Medicare, and Medicaid.

In 1993, Social Security is projected to surpass defense as the largest item in the federal budget. It now absorbs roughly one-fifth of all federal spending. The Social Security budget is expected to rise from its 1992 level of about $285 billion to almost $385 billion by 1998. Although Medicare and Medicaid are smaller programs than Social Security, their cost is rising even more rapidly. The federal government, which provides health insurance for the elderly through Medicare and for the poor through Medicaid, currently covers a little less than half of the nation's total health care bill. According to the final budget prepared by the Bush administration, the cost of Medicare is expected to double between 1992 and the end of the decade. Spending for Medicaid will grow even more rapidly.

WHY CHANGES ARE NECESSARY

Few people question the importance of keeping the Social Security system intact. But because the system is growing out of proportion to the nation's ability to pay for it, say advocates of this view, Social Security must be reexamined and its costs contained.

As Peter Peterson points out, if benefits are not limited, the Social Security payroll tax, which is currently 13 percent of wages, could rise as high as 40 percent by the year 2030. That is likely to create real tension between the generations. As Peterson says, "At some point, young workers will simply refuse to pay the crushing taxes required to support their elders."

Another reason benefits must be adjusted, say proponents of this choice, is that Social Security distributes benefits to people who neither need nor deserve public subsidies. Over the length of their retirement years, average retirees get three to six times more in benefits than they and their employers paid into the fund.

According to the Congressional Research Service, a typical man retiring in 1991 who paid the maximum amount of Social Security taxes during his working years can expect to receive a $32,000 subsidy during his retirement years. Advocates of this choice are convinced that there is no justification for generous public subsidies to elderly people who don't need them.

Advocates of this choice advance three proposals for trimming the cost of Social Security. One is to reduce the cost-of-living adjustment. Currently, whenever the cost of living increases, Social Security benefits rise automatically by the same amount. This procedure, known as indexing, provides reassurance to retirees, many of whom depend on Social Security checks for the bulk of their income. But it also makes the program more costly and adds to the deficit. "Let us slaughter the sacred cow of indexing," says Peter Peterson, "which so many are now milking. Neither the nation's working people nor private pensioners are given 100 percent protection against inflation."

Social Security poster, 1935

A second proposal is to increase taxes on Social Security benefits for middle- and high-income families. Currently, Social Security benefits are taxable only if an elderly person's total income exceeds a certain level. If your income as an individual is more than $25,000, or if your income as a couple exceeds $32,000, 50 percent of your Social Security benefits are regarded as taxable income. As part of his deficit-reduction plan, President Clinton proposed taxing 85 percent of those benefits, which would affect about 1 in 5 retirees and raise about $30 billion over 5 years.

A third proposal favored by proponents of this choice would raise the retirement age. To make way for younger workers, Congress defined 65 as the mandatory age of retirement and declared that no one would be eligible to collect full benefits unless they stopped working. The average American who reaches age 65 can expect to live — and collect Social Security pension checks — for another 15-19 years, the equivalent of about 40 percent of a person's working life. Encouraging people to retire at age 65, in the words of sociologist Kingsley Davis, "is a luxury this nation is no longer able to afford."

A majority of the American public opposes changes in the Social Security system. Still, advocates of this choice are convinced that unless we reform the system and reduce its cost, it is unlikely that much progress can be made in reducing the federal deficit.

PAYING FOR HEALTH CARE

In the 1960s, the nation made an important commitment to the poor and elderly. By enacting the Medicaid and Medicare programs, the government agreed to provide health insurance to these two groups of Americans. Medicaid, which is jointly funded by the states and the federal government, provides medical services to the poor. Medicare, which workers support with a portion of their Social Security payroll taxes, is a federal health insurance program designed to cover the medical costs of those 65 and over.

In the 1960s, when these programs were started, Medicare and Medicaid seemed humane and affordable. But, Medicare and Medicaid are now the fastest-growing items in the federal budget. The combined cost of these programs is projected to rise from the 1992 level of $197 billion to $365 billion by 1997. If Medicare continues to grow at its current rate, it is expected by the year 2005 to be the largest single item in the federal budget, surpassing even Social Security.

The health care cost problem is widely recognized. Many people are convinced that the United States can no longer afford an open-ended commitment to provide the elderly and needy with health insurance, and that the cost of these programs must be trimmed.

Since the federal government pays roughly half the nation's total health care bill, nothing less than thorough reform of the system is likely to contain the cost of Medicare and Medicaid. Various proposals have been put forward to rein in public health care costs. Some say that Medicare patients should

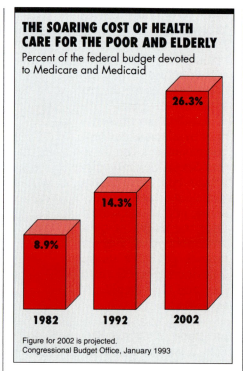

THE SOARING COST OF HEALTH CARE FOR THE POOR AND ELDERLY
Percent of the federal budget devoted to Medicare and Medicaid

8.9% — 1982
14.3% — 1992
26.3% — 2002

Figure for 2002 is projected.
Congressional Budget Office, January 1993

be required to use health care arrangements that contain costs, such as health maintenance organizations (HMOs). Others favor requiring elderly patients who can afford to pay for their medical care to do so.

If we continue in the current direction, says physician and essayist Lewis Thomas, we face "demographic disaster — a pile-up of the feeble and the infirm," as well as soaring public expenses for programs whose cost is virtually out of control.

WHAT CRITICS SAY

As defenders of entitlement programs see it, providing for individuals who are unable to provide for themselves, including the needy and the elderly, is a public responsibility. It would be irresponsible to justify cuts in entitlement programs in the name of reducing the federal deficit.

The fact that a large part of the entitlement budget goes to the elderly is no accident, say critics. Social Security and Medicare fill an important need

both for older people who are retired and their families. If these programs did not exist, young people would have to provide for their parents' economic well-being.

It is no surprise, say defenders of these programs, that large majorities of all ages oppose cutbacks in entitlement programs. Roughly three-quarters of all Americans reject the suggestion that benefits should be reduced for retirees in the future. Similarly, a majority rejects proposals to raise the retirement age as a way of reducing entitlement costs. After more than 50 years of being told that retirement begins at 65, many consider retirement at that age an inalienable right.

Although proposals to reduce Social Security — such as putting a one-year freeze on the cost-of-living adjustment — may seem reasonable, critics point out that they will harm those who are most dependent on Social Security. It is important to remember, say critics of cutbacks in entitlement spending, that many of the elderly get along on a very modest income. According to the House Ways and Means Committee, 28 percent of the nation's elderly families have incomes of under $10,000. For these individuals, Social Security payments provide, on average, about three-quarters of their income.

Defenders of Medicare and Medicaid have a similar concern. If spending on these programs were reduced, the poor and the elderly might be forced to pay more out of their own pockets, putting the burden of deficit reduction on the backs of people who are least able to support it.

As critics of this choice see it, government's first priority is to meet pressing needs and *then* figure out how to pay for them. In our eagerness to reduce the deficit, it would be a mistake to slash entitlement programs. Raising taxes is a fairer and more tolerable way of closing the budget gap. Having examined several ways in which federal spending could be reduced, let us consider the argument for reducing the deficit by raising additional revenues. ■

CHOICE #4
REVENUE SOLUTION:
NO SUCH THING AS A FREE LUNCH

"Our failure to levy taxes sufficient to cover public spending has undermined the economy and our international reputation. The fact is that we need higher taxes and can afford them. What is the fairest and most feasible way to raise new revenues?"

Every nation faces the problem of how to collect enough taxes to cover the cost of public programs. But Americans are even more reluctant to pay for government's cost than the people of most nations. After all, one of the most celebrated events in this nation's history was the Boston Tea Party, an anti-tax demonstration.

At the time of the Constitutional Convention, when hard-pressed state governments were printing paper money to cover their expenses, Alexander Hamilton, who became the first Secretary of the Treasury, appealed to his countrymen to understand why higher taxes were necessary. "How is it possible," he asked, "that a government half-supplied can provide for the security, advance the prosperity, or support the reputation of the commonwealth? How can it possess either energy or stability, dignity or credit, confidence at home or respectability abroad?"

Two centuries later, as proponents of our final choice point out, Hamilton's plea is more urgent and timely than ever. The failure of the federal government to levy sufficient taxes to cover public spending has undermined both the U.S. economy and America's

international reputation.

In 1991, the Organization of Economic Cooperation and Development (OECD) — a Paris-based group of wealthy nations — delivered a strong rebuke in a report that compared the tax rates and public debt of various nations. The report portrayed the United States as a rich, spoiled brat that refuses to take its tax medicine and, as a result of heavy borrowing, harms other nations and weakens the international economy. It pointed out that among the 24 wealthiest nations in the world, only Turkey collects a smaller percentage of its Gross Domestic Product than does the United States.

Few people propose to eliminate the deficit by relying entirely on tax increases. To close the $290 billion budget gap, individual income taxes would need to be raised by almost 50 percent. But many are convinced that higher taxes are the fairest and most realistic solution to controlling the deficit. In an

GARY HALLGREN

April 1991 broadcast of the "NBC Nightly News," commentator John Chancellor said, "The truth is that the U.S. needs higher taxes and can afford them. Some political leaders are now starting to say that. But until more say it, the country will remain in trouble."

Because there is strong public resistance to new taxes, most elected officials avoid speaking out in favor of them. In early 1992, when the nation faced the prospect of a record-high deficit, Congress was considering a tax cut for the middle class. Senator Warren Rudman, who soon after announced his retirement, delivered a blistering speech on the Senate floor. "How is it that we can stand on this floor and talk about doing anything that has even the slightest chance of adding a penny to the deficit?" asked Rudman. Time after time, he said, "Presidents and Congresses, Democrats and Republicans alike, have been unwilling to explain to the American people that there is no such thing as a free lunch."

TAX BURDEN

While federal revenues come from many different sources, over 90 percent of the federal tax dollar comes from just three sources. Nine cents out of each tax dollar collected by the federal government comes from taxes on corporations. The payroll taxes paid into social insurance programs such as Social Security and Medicare add 38 cents to the federal revenue dollar. Forty-four cents comes from individual income taxes.

Compared to other industrial nations, as advocates of this choice point out, the taxes Americans pay are quite modest. Even if a 5 percent sales tax were put into effect, or if income tax rates were increased by a few percentage points, Americans would still pay less than people in other industrial nations.

To proponents of the revenue solution, that is a crucial point. Although we demand roughly the same public services and programs that people in other industrial nations take for granted, we resist paying for them. The most straightforward explanation for chronic deficits is that we are undertaxed. Paying additional taxes is an honest way of paying the bill for big government. As long as we continue to finance national spending by running huge deficits, we're fooling ourselves.

Raising revenues is the best solution for reducing the deficit for another reason, say advocates of this choice. Reducing spending for specific programs hurts some groups more than others. Tax hikes, on the other hand, can be applied to everyone more or less equally. Raising additional revenues to close the budget gap, say advocates, forces us to face the question of how the burden of paying for public goods should be distributed — a question that the current habit of deficit spending allows us to avoid.

REVENUE-RAISING MENU

What measures should be taken to generate additional revenues? On Capitol Hill, various proposals have been considered recently for raising additional government revenues. Prominent items on the list include higher taxes on upper-income individuals, across-the-board increases in tax rates, and new consumption taxes.

In February 1993, in his first major economic address, President Clinton followed up on his campaign promise by proposing to raise the top rate — now 31 percent — to 36 percent for the wealthiest Americans. He also proposed a surtax for very wealthy individuals whose income exceeds $1 million.

A tax system is progressive to the extent that people who earn more are expected to pay a higher percentage of their earnings. Supporters of this option argue that since tax rates were dramatically reduced in 1981 for upper-bracket taxpayers, the system has been less progressive. In the words of Robert McIntyre, director of Citizens for Tax Justice, "Rich people are undertaxed based on what they can afford, what they used to pay, and what their counterparts pay in other countries."

Some proponents of this choice argue that since the budget gap is so large, it may be necessary to raise everyone's taxes. The current law defines three tax rates — 15 percent, 28 percent, and 31 percent — depending on your income. According to the CBO, increasing tax rates on ordinary income

THE FEDERAL TAX DOLLAR, 1992

Total Revenues: $1.09 Trillion

44¢
INDIVIDUAL INCOME TAXES
$476 Billion

38¢
SOCIAL INSURANCE
$414 Billion

9¢
CORPORATE INCOME TAXES
$100 Billion

4¢
EXCISE TAXES
$46 Billion

5¢
OTHER RECEIPTS
$55 Billion

Congressional Budget Office, January 1993

"Time after time, presidents and Congresses, Democrats and Republicans alike, have been unwilling to explain to the American people that there is no such thing as a free lunch."

— Senator Warren Rudman

REVENUE RAISERS: INTRODUCING THE ENERGY TAX

A major new revenue source proposed by President Clinton as part of his deficit-reduction package is a levy on energy, designed to raise $22 billion a year by 1996. The energy tax would be based on the energy content of various fuels, as measured in BTUs (British thermal units).

An energy tax would raise the price of gasoline, natural gas, coal, and heating oil, as well as the price of manufactured goods whose production consumes energy. The tax would not apply to solar and wind energy.

Clinton believes that one of the virtues of a broad-based energy tax is that its burden would be spread evenly among most Americans. Taxes on individual forms of energy tend to burden certain groups disproportionately. A gas tax, for example, places a particular burden on those who drive long distances.

Energy taxes are also favored by many environmentalists because they encourage consumers to restrain their use of carbon-based fuels, which are a chief cause of global warming.

The Clinton administration estimates that, if an energy tax were adopted, a typical family of four would pay about $120 more each year in direct taxes for the gas and electricity they use to heat and light their homes, as well as for gasoline. A typical family would also pay about $200 a year in indirect costs passed on by businesses whose energy costs are higher.

Critics, like Charles DiBona, president of the American Petroleum Institute, believe the cost of an energy tax would be significantly higher. According to DiBona, the overall cost of the tax to a typical family would be roughly $500 a year, not $320 as administration officials projected.

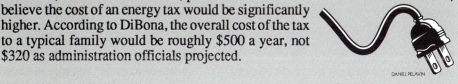

DANIEL PELAVIN

by approximately 7 percent — to 16 percent, 30 percent, and 33 percent — would add $175 billion to the federal treasury over the next five years.

Advocates of the revenue solution also support measures to raise excise taxes on cigarettes and alcohol, as a way of discouraging consumption of these products and raising revenues. The CBO estimates that doubling the excise tax on cigarettes, which is now 24 cents a pack, would generate $3 billion per year.

Some proponents of this choice favor more ambitious measures to raise revenues, such as a 50-cents-a-gallon increase in gas taxes, or a federal consumption tax. Similar to state sales taxes, national consumption taxes would increase the cost of most goods. To keep the consumption tax fair,

essential items such as food and medicine would be exempted. Even if such items were exempt, a 5 percent national sales tax would generate an estimated $60-70 billion a year.

WHAT CRITICS SAY

Polls show that the American public strongly opposes new taxes. A two-thirds majority is convinced that federal taxes are already too high. Even if there were popular support for raising taxes, critics are skeptical that additional revenues would be used to close the deficit. "Let's face it," says columnist Donald Lambro, "Congress will not use income from higher taxes to reduce the deficit or balance the budget. They will do what they have

always done when taxes are raised: spend it. Giving Congress more money by raising taxes is like giving drugs to a drug addict." Our goal, say critics, should be to achieve the lowest possible level of taxes and the utmost frugality in public spending.

Critics are especially concerned about soaking the rich by levying even higher taxes on the wealthiest Americans. Households whose income is in the top 10 percent already pay more than half of all federal taxes. Placing a greater tax burden on the wealthy will discourage these individuals from saving and investing in new enterprises, thus hindering economic growth.

Critics are also concerned about consumption taxes. A consumption tax would raise the price of nearly every purchase, thus creating a drag on the economy. Critics also note that consumption taxes are inherently regressive. Since poor individuals spend a greater portion of their income on consumption, such a tax would affect them disproportionately.

Whenever special taxes are levied, say critics, the people who pay them feel unfairly burdened. That happened in 1982, when Congress passed measures to increase the gas tax and highway user fees. In protest, the trucking industry staged a nationwide strike, which interrupted the transport of many products and sparked violent incidents across the country.

Similarly, say critics, a 50-cents-a-gallon increase in gas taxes would be particularly harmful to individuals in sparsely populated regions of the country. "This would be a killer for North Dakota," says Governor Edward T. Schafer. "In a rural state, a lot of people depend on their cars not only to get to their jobs but during the harvest season to get supplies. An increase in gas taxes would affect people here a lot harder."

Critics of the revenue solution conclude that the best way to balance the budget is not to require individuals to pay more in taxes, but to pare down government spending. ■

DEBTOR NATION:
BAD HABITS, HARD CHOICES

"Each day we put off the task of balancing the budget, it gets $1 billion harder. We must find some common ground for action on a broadly acceptable deficit-reduction package that spreads the pain and sacrifice."

In a recent book of essays about public life, *Around the Cragged Hill*, George Kennan, an influential analyst of American foreign policy for half a century, turns his attention to the nation's domestic ills. What he sees is sad and sobering. The United States, says Kennan, is in "critical shape" because Americans have become "a people of bad social habits." One source of the frailties of the American system, in his view, is the constant need of politicians to get reelected, which deters them from unpleasant but necessary acts of public stewardship. After pondering various social ills, including the national debt, Kennan concludes that "one has no choice but to question the adequacy of democracy itself as a means of responding to today's challenges."

There is no disputing the fact that 12-digit deficits and a 13-digit national debt are evidence of bad social habits. Interest payments have become a black hole, which sucks up an increasingly large portion of the federal budget, making it harder for government to provide programs and services that the public expects. As Kennan suggests, indebtedness poses a severe test of a democratic system in which specific, short-term interests crowd out concern for the long-term public interest.

The United States is faced with a fundamental decision. We can continue to spend far in excess of government revenues, borrowing more and more to make up the difference. If nothing is done to reduce spending or raise new revenues, annual deficits are projected to rise to $650 billion — more than twice their current size — over the next decade. As a result, says CBO head Robert Reischauer, "the U.S. economy will slip out of world-class status," and our children and grandchildren will be forced to pay for our profligacy.

Or we can begin to make a fundamental adjustment by increasing revenues and decreasing spending. By accepting certain kinds of sacrifice and discomfort, we can avoid the certainty of even more painful choices and declining economic prospects in the future.

As we have seen, four prescriptions for deficit reduction have been put forward. Each of the four strategies rests on certain assertions about values — how much government we want, for what purposes, and what we are willing to pay for it. Each strategy would impose certain costs and sacrifices.

Advocates of our first choice favor closing the budget gap by reducing discretionary spending, even if that means doing without programs and services that many Americans take for granted.

Advocates of our second choice favor deep cuts in defense spending, even if that means giving up our accustomed role as superpower, and the loss of hundreds of thousands of jobs in defense-related industries.

Advocates of our third choice would trim the budget by scaling down entitlement programs, even if that means learning to live with fewer benefits from such programs as Medicare and Social Security.

Advocates of our fourth choice would close the budget gap by raising revenues, even if that means paying more out of our own pockets for new taxes.

In an important respect, the debt debate is about how to distribute the costs and sacrifices associated with each of these strategies so that no group feels the budget is being balanced mainly at its expense.

PROMPT ACTION

Regardless of what the deficit-reduction package consists of, there is a growing sense that action must be taken. In June 1992, in testimony to the Senate Subcommittee on Deficits and Debt Management, Charles Bowsher, Comptroller General of the United States, underlined the importance of prompt action. "The question facing policymakers," he said, "is not whether to reduce the deficit, only when and how. In the face of widening deficits, inaction is not a sustainable policy."

The debt debate begins with the recognition that our unwillingness to deal with the problem is already imposing costs of various kinds. As Sam Nunn and Pete Domenici comment in their introduction to the report of the Strengthening of America Commission, "The question is whether we choose the sacrifices or whether they choose us."

Just before he took office, president-elect Clinton promised decisive action on the deficit. "We all understand the price we're going to have to pay if we continue with this deficit," said Clinton at an economic summit meeting convened a month after his election.

At the start of the Clinton administration, the American public was optimistic that the new administration would succeed in various areas. A New York Times/CBS News poll showed that a 66 percent majority thought Clinton would take steps to provide health insurance to all Americans. Six out of ten Americans thought the new administration would create a significant number of new jobs. But only 26 percent thought the Clinton administration would be able to reduce the deficit significantly.

Considering how often elected officials have announced a new plan or reached a new agreement that promised to reduce the deficit, and then failed to

do so, a certain skepticism about the Clinton administration's promises to control the deficit is understandable. As Harold Figgie, Jr. and Gerald Swanson comment in a harsh account called *Bankruptcy 1995: The Coming Collapse of America*, "Most of the decisions and actions taken in Washington in the name of deficit reduction have reduced nothing but the deficit's visibility."

THE PUBLIC'S RESPONSIBILITY

It is easy to blame leaders for their inaction on the deficit. In an important respect, however, this misses the point because it fails to acknowledge the public's responsibility for the problem. Some say that the cause of the problem is that elected officials are out of touch with the citizenry, oblivious to their concern about deficit spending. It is more accurate to turn that explanation around. The reason for huge deficits is that elected officials in Washington accurately *reflect* the conflicting impulses of the public.

"The reason the federal government persistently spends more than it has," writes columnist Anthony Lewis, "is that we the people want it that way. We think we are entitled to a free federal

lunch. We demand that our political leaders give us the benefits — and then denounce them for not balancing the budget."

Polls show majority support for increased government spending in dozens of areas — including ameliorating poverty, improving public education, fighting drugs, protecting the nation's health, improving public transportation, and protecting the environment. Similarly, many people believe it is unwise, even dangerous, to reduce military spending much below current levels. In only a few areas is there majority support for decreased spending.

At the same time, there is little support for the taxes required to pay for an ambitious package of government programs and services. In recent polls, large majorities of Americans reject such revenue raisers as a modest hike in income tax rates or a 10-cents-a-gallon hike in gas taxes.

In the short run, most Americans are less afraid of the deficit than they are of what government might do to reduce the deficit, such as cutting popular programs or imposing new taxes. In the words of E. J. Dionne, Jr., reporter for the *Washington Post,* "There is a large

STEVE BENSON/TRIBUNE MEDIA SERVICES

constituency for spending. There is a large constituency for cutting taxes. There is no constituency for deficit reduction. The result is political gridlock."

Consider what happened on Capitol Hill in April 1992, when a bipartisan group of senators — Warren Rudman, Pete Domenici, Sam Nunn, and Charles Robb — tried to restrain the growth of federal spending by proposing a cap on overall entitlement growth. To make it politically palatable, they proposed to exempt Social Security. The senators portrayed the bill as the kind of action necessary to keep deficits from skyrocketing over the next few years. Senator Charles Robb went out of his way to explain that "We do not seek to end entitlements, or even to reduce them," he said. "We do, however, believe that it is necessary to restrain their growth."

However necessary such measures may be, the senators' proposed cap on entitlement triggered off a firestorm of opposition. Within two hours of the first detailed discussion of the proposal, the sponsors' offices were deluged with irate messages. The messages came, said Domenici, "from all over the country, saying this is going to hurt a veterans' group, this is going to hurt people on welfare, this is going to hurt seniors on Medicare."

"We were inundated," said William Hoagland, staff director of the Senate Budget Committee. "Just about every interest group you can think of was strongly opposed." The American Association of Retired Persons called the proposal a "direct attack." The Committee for Education Funding called it "unconscionable." The American Federation of Government Employees called it "unfair." The Veterans of Foreign Wars called it "totally unjust." And the American Postal Workers Union called it "irresponsible and simpleminded." Faced with outraged opposition and the prospect of almost certain defeat, the bill's sponsors withdrew their plan — and the deficit continued its inexorable rise.

HONEST TALK, REALISTIC SOLUTIONS

As things stand, says Peter Peterson, "we have a Catch-22. Politicians won't lead because they consider it suicidal to do the right thing. The people, growing more pessimistic about the future, are in turn tuning out the politicians. We need to reverse this situation and create an environment in which politicians and the public can support each other in saying and doing the right thing."

The question is not only whether elected officials are willing to talk honestly about the need for sacrifice to close the budget gap, but whether the public is prepared to listen, and accept measures that impose short-term pain for long-term gain.

If, as Anthony Lewis suggests, "the real source of the budget disaster lies in public desires and illusions," the first step toward resolving the budget impasse is for millions of Americans to gain a realistic understanding of the extent of the problem, and what kinds of measures are needed to deal with it. An infinite variety of program cuts and revenue increases could be used to close the budget gap. But several things

are clear. The deficit won't be reduced substantially merely by eliminating waste, fraud, and abuse. Neither will the budget be balanced by cutting just those programs that many people don't like — such as foreign aid — while leaving popular programs such as Medicare and Social Security untouched.

At a time of $300 billion deficits, anyone who wants to balance the budget has to consider how to cut federal spending and increase government revenues at the same time. Devising a way to do so without harming the needy, endangering national security, or damaging the nation's economic prospects is a truly difficult task.

If we are to make any progress in solving this problem, both citizens and elected officials will have to end what Warren Rudman calls a "conspiracy of silence" about the public debt. The problem won't be solved until elected officials are convinced this is what their constituents demand. If the new administration is to succeed in this respect, the American public will have to show that we understand the problem and that we are ready to accept a fairly shared solution.■

For Further Reading

The basic sources for budgetary information are *The Budget of the United States Government*, prepared annually by the president's Office of Management and Budget, and two Congressional Budget Office reports, *Reducing the Deficit: Spending and Revenue Options*, and *The Economic and Budget Outlook*, both issued annually. See also a June 1992 report from the U.S. General Accounting Office, *Budget Policy: Prompt Action Necessary to Avert Long-Term Damage to the Economy*, which shows how four different courses of action would play out over the next 30 years.

For an overall analysis of the deficit problem and its significance, see Benjamin Friedman's *Day of Reckoning: The Consequences of American Economic Policy Under Reagan and After* (New York: Random House, 1988). For a blueprint of how the deficit might be reduced, see H. Ross Perot's *United We Stand: How We Can Take Back Our Country* (New York: Hyperion, 1992). In *Restoring America's Future: Preparing the Nation for the 21st Century* (Washington, D.C.: House Budget Committee, 1991), Budget Director Leon Panetta offers a ten-year plan for reducing the deficit and restoring economic prosperity. *The Strengthening of America Commission First Report* (Washington, D.C.: Center for Strategic and International Studies, 1992) outlines a seven-point budget plan that calls for spending cuts in several different areas as well as tax increases.

For a detailed blueprint of the Clinton administration's deficit-reduction package, see *A Vision of Change for America* (Washington, D.C.: The White House, February 1993), available from the Government Printing Office.

Lawrence Haas' article, "Never Say Die," in *National Journal*, March 28, 1992, describes the efforts of the Bush administration to cut discretionary spending and examines why such efforts have not succeeded in the past. For a fresh, well-written analysis of

problems that should be federal responsibilities, and problems that are better addressed in other ways, see Alice Rivlin's *Reviving the American Dream: The Economy, the States and the Federal Government* (Washington, D.C.: Brookings, 1992).

On the topic of defense spending and how much it can be reduced, see William W. Kaufmann and John D. Steinbruner's *Decisions for Defense: Prospects for a New Order* (Washington, D.C.: Brookings, 1992); Earl C. Ravenal's *Designing Defense for a New World Order* (Washington, D.C.: Cato Institute, 1991); Stephen Daggett's "U.S. Forces Overseas: How Many, Where, and What Do They Cost?" in the April/May 1992 issue of *CRS Review*; Defense Secretary Les Aspin's report, *An Approach to Sizing American Conventional Forces for the Post-Soviet Era* (Washington, D.C.: House Armed Services Committee, 1992); Keith Berner's report, *Defense Budget for FY 1993: Data Summary* (Washington, D.C.: Congressional Research Service, March 1992); W.Y. Smith's "U.S. National Security After the Cold War," in *Washington Quarterly*, Vol.

ROB SAUNDERS

15, No. 4, Fall 1992; and Jack Beatty's article, "A Post-Cold War Budget," which appeared in *The Atlantic Monthly*, February 1990.

For an analysis of entitlement programs and their rising cost, see Peter G. Peterson's *On Borrowed Time: How the Growth in Entitlement Spending*

Threatens America's Future (New York: ICS Press, 1988). See also an article by Neil Howe and Phillip Longman, "The Next New Deal," in the April 1992 issue of *The Atlantic Monthly*. For arguments against cutting back entitlements, see reports and press briefings from the National Committee to Preserve Social Security and Medicare.

In *The Rise and Fall of the Great Powers*, historian Paul Kennedy argues that the fate of various nations has hinged on their ability to marshal public resources through taxation. For an analysis of federal tax policy, see Herbert Stein's *Tax Policy in the 21st Century* (New York: Wiley, 1988).

Three national organizations focus on deficit reduction. The Committee for a Responsible Federal Budget is committed to educating the public on the need for fiscal responsibility. The Concord Coalition encourages grass roots support for deficit reduction. A Washington-based grass roots campaign, Lead or Leave, which focuses on implications of deficit spending for those currently in their twenties, refers to itself as "a generational revolt against politics as usual."

Acknowledgments

We would like to express our appreciation to the people who helped choose this year's issues, and took part in discussions about how to frame them. Once again, David Mathews and Daniel Yankelovich provided guidance and support. Our colleagues Jean Johnson, Jon Rye Kinghorn, Robert Kingston, Patrick Scully, and Deborah Wadsworth played a valuable role in refining the framework and clarifying the presentation.

Special thanks to the following individuals, who reviewed the manuscript and offered helpful suggestions: Martha Phillips at the Concord Coalition; Bill Cox and Stephen Daggett of the Congressional Research Service; and Paul Leonard of the Center for Budget and Policy Priorities.

NATIONAL ISSUES FORUMS

The National Issues Forums (NIF) program consists of locally initiated Forums and study circles which bring citizens together in communities throughout the nation for non-partisan discussions about public issues. In these Forums, the traditional town meeting concept is re-created. Each fall and winter, three issues of particular concern are addressed in these groups. The results are then shared with policymakers.

More than 3,000 civic and education organizations — high schools and colleges, libraries, service organizations, religious groups, and other types of groups — convene Forums and study circles in their communities as part of the National Issues Forums. Each participating organization assumes ownership of the program, adapting the NIF approach and materials to its own mission and to the needs of the local community. In this sense, there is no one type of NIF program. There are many varieties, all locally directed and financed.

Here are answers to some of the most frequently asked questions about the National Issues Forums:

WHAT HAPPENS IN FORUMS?

The goal of Forums and study circles is to stimulate and sustain a certain kind of conversation — a genuinely useful conversation that moves beyond the bounds of partisan politics and the airing of grievances to mutually acceptable responses to common problems. Distinctively, Forums invite discussion about each of several choices, along with their cost and the main arguments for and against them. Forum moderators encourage participants to examine their values and preferences — as individuals and as community members — and apply them to specific issues.

CAN I PARTICIPATE IF I'M NOT WELL INFORMED ABOUT THE ISSUE?

To discuss public issues, citizens need to grasp the underlying problem or dilemma, and they should understand certain basic facts and trends. But it isn't necessary to know a great deal about an issue. NIF discussions focus on what public actions should be taken. That's a matter of judgment that requires collective deliberation. The most important thing to ponder and discuss is the kernel of convictions on which each alternative is based. The task of the National Issues Forums is not to help participants acquire a detailed knowledge of the issue but to help people sort out conflicting principles and preferences, to find out where they agree and disagree and work toward common understandings.

ISN'T ONE PERSON'S OPINION AS GOOD AS ANOTHER'S?

Public judgment differs from personal opinion. It arises when people sort out their values and work through hard choices. Public judgment reflects people's views once they have an opportunity to confront an issue seriously, consider the arguments for and against various positions, and come to terms with the consequences of their beliefs.

ARE FORUM PARTICIPANTS EXPECTED TO AGREE UPON A COURSE OF ACTION?

A fundamental challenge in a democratic nation is sustaining a consensus about a broad direction of public action without ignoring or denying the diversity of individual preferences. Forums do not attempt to achieve complete agreement. Rather, their goal is to help people see which interests are shareable and which are not. A Forum moderator once described the common ground in these words: "Here are five statements that were made in our community Forum. Not everyone agreed with all of them. But there is nothing in them that we couldn't live with."

WHAT'S THE POINT OF ONE MORE BULL SESSION?

Making choices is hard work. It requires something more than talking about public issues. "Talking about" is what we do every day. We talk about the weather, or our friends, or the government. But the "choice work" that takes place in Forum discussions involves weighing alternatives and considering the consequences of various courses of action. It means accepting certain choices even if they aren't entirely consistent with what we want, and even if the cost is higher than we imagined. Forum participants learn how to work through issues together. That means using talk to discover, not just to persuade or advocate.

DO THE FORUMS LEAD TO POLITICAL ACTION?

Neither local convenors nor the National Issues Forums as a whole advocate partisan positions or specific solutions. The Forums' purpose is to influence the political process in a more fundamental way. Before elected officials decide upon specific proposals, they need to know what kinds of initiatives the public favors. As President Carter once said, "Government cannot set goals and it cannot define our vision." The purpose of the Forums is to provide an occasion for people to decide what broad direction public action should take.

PRE-FORUM BALLOT

THE $4 TRILLION DEBT:
TOUGH CHOICES ABOUT SOARING FEDERAL DEFICITS

One of the reasons people participate in the National Issues Forums is that they want leaders to know how they feel about the issues. So that we can present your thoughts and feelings about this issue, we'd like you to fill out this ballot before you attend Forum meetings (or before you read this book if you buy it elsewhere) and a second ballot after the Forum. Before answering any of the questions, make up a three-digit number and fill it in the box below.

The moderator of your local Forum will ask you to hand in this ballot at the end of the session. If you cannot attend the meeting, send the completed ballot to National Issues Forums, 100 Commons Road, Dayton, Ohio 45459-2777.

Fill in your three-digit number here. ☐

---

1. Here are four views about why the U.S. has such large deficits. How important do you think each one is? Give the most important reason a 1. Give the next most important a 2. Give the third most important a 3. Give the least important a 4.

   We have large deficits because:

   a. Government spends a lot of money on wasteful agencies and programs. ☐

   b. We are spending too much money on defense. ☐

   c. Costly entitlement programs such as Social Security and Medicare keep growing whether we can afford them or not. ☐

   d. Taxes are not high enough to pay for all the government programs we want. ☐

---

2. How do you feel about each of these approaches to reducing the U.S. deficit?

	Favor	Oppose	Not Sure
a. We should spend less money on parks, highways, and the space program, **EVEN IF** that means investing less money in our country's future.	☐	☐	☐
b. We should make deep cuts in defense spending, **EVEN IF** that means giving up our role as a superpower and doing away with thousands of jobs.	☐	☐	☐
c. We should cut spending on entitlement programs, **EVEN IF** that means fewer benefits for the poor and the elderly.	☐	☐	☐
d. We should raise taxes, **EVEN IF** that means adding to the burden of most taxpayers.	☐	☐	☐

2A. Look again at the approaches you **opposed** in Question 2. Are there any you could live with if other people favored those approaches? If so, which one(s)?

   a. ☐
   b. ☐
   c. ☐
   d. ☐

NATIONAL ISSUES FORUMS

(over)

3. Here are some views people have about each choice. How do you feel about them?

	Agree	Disagree	Not Sure

Choice #1: Discretionary Spending: A Guided Tour of Federal Programs

	Agree	Disagree	Not Sure
a. We can successfully balance the budget by getting rid of waste, fraud, and abuse.	☐	☐	☐
b. If we cut spending on certain public programs, many Americans, especially the poor, would not get services they depend on.	☐	☐	☐
c. We should cut government spending on services such as the post office that could be better run by private businesses.	☐	☐	☐

Choice #2: Defense Decisions: How Much More Can Be Cut?

	Agree	Disagree	Not Sure
a. Since the Cold War has ended, we can afford to make larger cuts in the defense budget.	☐	☐	☐
b. The U.S. must maintain a strong defense because there is still much disorder in the world.	☐	☐	☐
c. Instead of being the world's policeman, the U.S. should share peacekeeping costs and duties with other nations.	☐	☐	☐

Choice #3: The Uncontrollables: Putting a Lid on Entitlements

	Agree	Disagree	Not Sure
a. Unless the growth of entitlement programs such as Social Security and Medicare is controlled, we won't have enough money for other programs and services.	☐	☐	☐
b. Limiting spending on entitlement programs such as Social Security and Medicare would unfairly burden the poor and the elderly.	☐	☐	☐
c. The retirement age should be raised above 65, to reduce Social Security costs and keep healthy older people in the work force.	☐	☐	☐

Choice #4: Revenue Solution: No Such Thing as a Free Lunch

	Agree	Disagree	Not Sure
a. Raising taxes is the fairest way to reduce the federal deficit because everyone would share the burden.	☐	☐	☐
b. Special taxes such as a gas tax would unfairly burden people with lower incomes.	☐	☐	☐
c. Government should adopt a national sales tax to help reduce the federal deficit.	☐	☐	☐

4. Which of these age groups are you in?

a. Under 18 ☐   **b.** 18 to 29 ☐   **c.** 30 to 44 ☐
d. 45 to 64 ☐   **e.** over 64 ☐

5. Are you a:

a. Man ☐   **b.** Woman ☐

6. Do you consider yourself:

a. White ☐
b. Black or African-American ☐
c. Hispanic ☐
d. Asian ☐
e. Other (Specify:_____) ☐

7. Have you completed:

a. Grade school or less ☐
b. Some high school ☐
c. High school ☐
d. Vocational/technical school ☐
e. Some college ☐
f. College ☐
g. Postgraduate work ☐

8. Do you live in the:

a. Northeast ☐   **b.** South ☐
c. Midwest ☐   **d.** West ☐
e. Southwest ☐

9. What is your ZIP CODE?_____

POST-FORUM BALLOT

THE $4 TRILLION DEBT:
TOUGH CHOICES ABOUT SOARING FEDERAL DEFICITS

Now that you've had a chance to read the book or attend a Forum discussion we'd like to know what you think about this issue. Your opinions, along with thousands of others who participated in this year's Forums, will be reflected in a summary report prepared for participants as well as elected officials and policymakers working on this problem. Some of these questions are the same as those you answered earlier. Before answering any of the questions, write the same three-digit number in the box below.

Please hand this to the Forum leader at the end of the session, or mail it to National Issues Forums, 100 Commons Road, Dayton, Ohio 45459-2777.

Fill in your three-digit number here. ☐

---

1. Here are four views about why the U.S. has such large deficits. How important do you think each one is? Give the most important reason a 1. Give the next most important a 2. Give the third most important a 3. Give the least important a 4.

   We have large deficits because:

   a. Government spends a lot of money on wasteful agencies and programs. ☐

   b. We are spending too much money on defense. ☐

   c. Costly entitlement programs such as Social Security and Medicare keep growing whether we can afford them or not. ☐

   d. Taxes are not high enough to pay for all the government programs we want. ☐

---

2. How do you feel about each of these approaches to reducing the U.S. deficit?

	Favor	Oppose	Not Sure
a. We should spend less money on parks, highways, and the space program, **EVEN IF** that means investing less money in our country's future.	☐	☐	☐
b. We should make deep cuts in defense spending, **EVEN IF** that means giving up our role as a superpower and doing away with thousands of jobs.	☐	☐	☐
c. We should cut spending on entitlement programs, **EVEN IF** that means fewer benefits for the poor and the elderly.	☐	☐	☐
d. We should raise taxes, **EVEN IF** that means adding to the burden of most taxpayers.	☐	☐	☐

2A. Look again at the approaches you **opposed** in Question 2. Are there any you could live with if other people favored those approaches? If so, which one(s)?

   a. ☐
   b. ☐
   c. ☐
   d. ☐

NATIONAL ISSUES FORUMS

(over)

3. Here are some views people have about each choice. How do you feel about them?

	Agree	Disagree	Not Sure

Choice #1: Discretionary Spending: A Guided Tour of Federal Programs

	Agree	Disagree	Not Sure
a. We can successfully balance the budget by getting rid of waste, fraud, and abuse.	☐	☐	☐
b. If we cut spending on certain public programs, many Americans, especially the poor, would not get services they depend on.	☐	☐	☐
c. We should cut government spending on services such as the post office that could be better run by private businesses.	☐	☐	☐

Choice #2: Defense Decisions: How Much More Can Be Cut?

	Agree	Disagree	Not Sure
a. Since the Cold War has ended, we can afford to make larger cuts in the defense budget.	☐	☐	☐
b. The U.S. must maintain a strong defense because there is still much disorder in the world.	☐	☐	☐
c. Instead of being the world's policeman, the U.S. should share peacekeeping costs and duties with other nations.	☐	☐	☐

Choice #3: The Uncontrollables: Putting a Lid on Entitlements

	Agree	Disagree	Not Sure
a. Unless the growth of entitlement programs such as Social Security and Medicare is controlled, we won't have enough money for other programs and services.	☐	☐	☐
b. Limiting spending on entitlement programs such as Social Security and Medicare would unfairly burden the poor and the elderly.	☐	☐	☐
c. The retirement age should be raised above 65, to reduce Social Security costs and keep healthy older people in the work force.	☐	☐	☐

Choice #4: Revenue Solution: No Such Thing as a Free Lunch

	Agree	Disagree	Not Sure
a. Raising taxes is the fairest way to reduce the federal deficit because everyone would share the burden.	☐	☐	☐
b. Special taxes such as a gas tax would unfairly burden people with lower incomes.	☐	☐	☐
c. Government should adopt a national sales tax to help reduce the federal deficit.	☐	☐	☐

4. Now that you have talked about the deficit, has your understanding of this issue:

- **a.** increased a lot ☐
- **b.** increased a little ☐
- **c.** not increased at all ☐
- **d.** not sure ☐

5. Has your understanding of **other people's** views on this issue:

- **a.** increased a lot ☐
- **b.** increased a little ☐
- **c.** not increased at all ☐
- **d.** not sure ☐

4A. If your understanding has increased at all, in what ways has it increased?

5A. If your understanding of **other people's** views has increased at all, in what ways has it increased?

6. What is your ZIP CODE?_____

NATIONAL ISSUES FORUMS
Order Form

ISSUE BOOKS (REGULAR AND ABRIDGED) $2.95 each	QTY	TOTAL

The Poverty Puzzle: What Should Be Done to Help the Poor?*
Regular Edition, 0-8403-8651-6
Abridged Edition, 0-8403-8652-4
The $4 Trillion Debt: Tough Choices about Soaring Federal Deficits*
Regular Edition, 0-8403-8653-2
Abridged Edition, 0-8403-8654-0
Health Care Cost Crunch: Why Costs Have Exploded, What Can Be Done* (Tentative Title)
Regular Edition, 0-8403-8656-7
Abridged Edition, 0-8403-8657-5

* Available August 1993

Education: How Do We Get the Results We Want?
Regular Edition, 0-8403-8138-7   ($3.50 each)
Issue in Brief, 0-8403-8139-5   (25 for $10.00)
People and Politics: Who Should Govern?
Regular Edition, 0-8403-8091-7
Abridged Edition, 0-8403-8212-X
The Health Care Crisis: Containing Costs, Expanding Coverage
Regular Edition, 0-8403-7432-1
Abridged Edition, 0-8403-7433-X
Criminal Violence: What Direction Now for the War on Crime?
Regular Edition, 0-8403-7435-6
Abridged Edition, 0-8403-7436-4
Prescription for Prosperity: Four Paths to Economic Renewal
Regular Edition, 0-8403-7438-0
Abridged Edition, 0-8403-7439-9
Energy Options: Finding a Solution to the Power Predicament
Regular Edition, 0-8403-6923-9
Abridged Edition, 0-8403-6926-3
The Boundaries of Free Speech: How Free Is Too Free?
Regular Edition, 0-8403-6924-7
Abridged Edition, 0-8403-6927-1
America's Role in the World: New Risks, New Realities
Regular Edition, 0-8403-6925-5
Abridged Edition, 0-8403-6928-X
The Battle over Abortion: Seeking Common Ground in a Divided Nation
Regular Edition, 0-8403-5937-3
Abridged Edition, 0-8403-5940-3
Regaining the Competitive Edge: Are We Up to the Job?
Regular Edition, 0-8403-5938-1
Abridged Edition, 0-8403-5941-1
Remedies for Racial Inequality: Why Progress Has Stalled, What Should Be Done
Regular Edition, 0-8403-5939-X
Abridged Edition, 0-8403-5942-X
Growing Up at Risk
Regular Edition, 0-8403-6028-2
Abridged Edition, 0-8403-6029-0
The Day Care Dilemma: Who Should Be Responsible for the Children?
Regular Edition, 0-8403-5264-6
Abridged Edition, 0-8403-5265-4
The Drug Crisis: Public Strategies for Breaking the Habit
Regular Edition, 0-8403-5270-0
Abridged Edition, 0-8403-5271-9
The Environment at Risk: Responding to Growing Dangers
Regular Edition, 0-8403-5267-0
Abridged Edition, 0-8403-5268-9
Health Care for the Elderly: Moral Dilemmas, Mortal Choices
Regular Edition, 0-8403-4796-0
Abridged Edition, 0-8403-4797-9
Coping with AIDS: The Public Response to the Epidemic
Regular Edition, 0-8403-4837-1
Abridged Edition, 0-8403-4838-X

VIDEOCASSETTES (VHS or 3/4" FORMAT) $35.00 each	QTY	TOTAL

VIDEO I*: The Poverty Puzzle, The $4 Trillion Debt, Health Care Cost Crunch (Tentative Title) _____ _____

VIDEO H: Education, 0-8403-8140-9 ($15.00 each) _____ _____

VIDEO G: The Health Care Crisis, Criminal Violence, Prescription for Prosperity, People and Politics, 0-8403-7441-0 _____ _____

VIDEO F: Energy Options, Boundaries of Free Speech, America's Role in the World, 0-8403-6955-7 _____ _____

VIDEO E: The Battle over Abortion, Regaining the Competitive Edge, Racial Inequality, Growing Up at Risk, 0-8403-5946-2 _____ _____

VIDEO D: Day Care Dilemma, Drug Crisis, Environment at Risk, 0-8403-8291-3 _____ _____

VIDEO C: Public Debt, Coping with AIDS, Health Care for the Elderly, 0-8403-4843-6 _____ _____

* Available August 1993

TOTAL AMOUNT DUE $_____

CALL TOLL FREE:

To order: 1-800-338-5578 (Fax 1-800-346-2377)

or

Fill in the information below and send to:

KENDALL/HUNT PUBLISHING COMPANY
2460 Kerper Boulevard, P.O. Box 539, Dubuque, Iowa 52004-0539

Name _____

Organization _____

Address _____

City _____ State/Zip _____

Phone: _____

❑ Charge my account:

_____ American Express Account No.: _____

_____ VISA MC Bank- _____

_____ MasterCard Expiration date _____

Signature _____

(required for all charges)

❑ Check enclosed

❑ Bill me (plus shipping and handling)